The Path to Positivity:

A Blueprint for Self-Improvement

Edward R. Anderson

Contents

Defining the Blueprint for Positive Transformation

The journey of personal transformation begins with self-reflection. Take time to understand your beliefs about change through journaling, meditation, and examining past experiences that shaped your perspectives. Clearly define your core values that provide the compass for growth. Ask probing questions and explore philosophical viewpoints to unearth motivations and assumptions. Find balance between accepting your current self while still aspiring for improvement.

Your values serve as guiding principles for behavior and decisions. Identify values aligned with your authentic self, integrate them into choices, and undertake change consistent with your beliefs. Aspirations represent your vision of your future self. Set intrinsic goals focused on self-fulfillment. Develop a clear picture of your desired growth, which fuels resilience when challenges arise.

Cultivate self-awareness, the cornerstone of personal evolution. Reflect mindfully on thoughts, emotions and behaviors to recognize patterns and adapt to change. This self-understanding provides a compass to guide intentional betterment. Approach positive thinking by examining the link between thoughts, feelings and actions. Discover practical strategies for setting goals, building resilience and fostering a growth mindset.

Share relatable stories showing positive change is attainable. Emphasize self-empowerment and taking ownership over your development. Ensure insights gained provide a solid base. Prompt reflection on values, dreams and the meaning of transformation. Adopt a holistic perspective on how positive changes in one area impact overall well-being. The journey of change requires understanding yourself before you can become your best self.

A brief story of how I became a better me;

When I turned 40, I realized I was deeply unhappy with my life. My marriage had grown stale, my job unfulfilling. Each day blurred into the next without passion or purpose. I knew something had to change but didn't know where to start.

I began by spending time in self-reflection, journaling to understand my core values. I uncovered a deep-seated need for meaning, creativity, and community. I explored philosophical perspectives on life's purpose, which resonated with my desire for something more.

Armed with this knowledge, I consciously worked to shift my mindset. I focused on personal growth and set goals aligned with my values like taking photography classes and volunteering at a local food bank. I started each day meditating, cultivating gratitude for small joys.

The changes came slowly at first. There were many setbacks and moments of doubt. But by persisting through challenges, I gradually transformed my life and mindset. One year later, I'm happier than I've ever been. I founded a nonprofit, reconnected with old friends, traveled, and found fulfillment in everyday moments. The journey continues, but by knowing and understanding myself, I've become the architect of my own transformation.

Chapter 1: The Power of Positivity

Understanding the Impact of Positive Thinking

Adopting a positive mindset can have a profoundly beneficial impact on various aspects of our mental, emotional, and physical health. At its core, optimism reduces stress levels by promoting more constructive attitudes when facing life's inevitable challenges. This builds emotional resilience, allowing positive thinkers to rebound quicker from adversity. Lower levels of anxiety and depression contribute to overall improved mental wellbeing.

Physically, positivity may strengthen the immune system to prevent illness and speed up recovery from surgery or disease. An upbeat outlook empowers problem-solving when obstacles arise by focusing on viable solutions. Positivity also breeds adaptability to change by embracing new possibilities.

Interpersonally, optimism enhances communication, conflict resolution, and meaningful connections by contributing to supportive environments. Achieving goals is also supported by enhanced motivation and perseverance driven by positivity. Some research indicates positive thinkers may even expect longer lifespans and experience an elevated quality of life.

Finally, positive thinking acknowledges the deep linkage between mind and body. A cheerful mindset helps minimize the mental and physical effects of stress through this holistic connection. Clearly, embracing positivity affects all areas of life. From cultivating resilience to nurturing relationships and achieving personal growth, the benefits of an optimistic mindset are far-reaching. Our minds have immense power to transform our reality when focused on the affirmative.

Overcoming Negativity and Cultivating Optimism

Negativity can permeate our thoughts and emotions, casting a shadow over life. Yet within us lies the capacity to transform this darkness into light by cultivating optimism. This journey begins with understanding negativity's roots. Ingrained thought patterns and core beliefs formed over time often reinforce pessimism, coloring our worldview.

To increase self-awareness, observe these habitual thoughts and irrational perspectives without judgement. Then actively challenge negativity by questioning its validity and substituting balanced, realistic thinking. Develop gratitude by regularly appreciating life's positives. Counteract self-criticism with positive affirmations. Minimize exposure to negative influences when possible.

Cultivating optimism involves nurturing a hopeful mindset. Set achievable goals and celebrate progress. Interpret challenges as opportunities for growth. Build a network of supportive relationships to encourage optimism. Focus on resolution over dwelling on problems. Engage in fulfilling activities that uplift your spirit.

To sustain optimism, consistency is key. Incorporate positive habits and mindset shifts into your daily routine. Adaptability helps maintain positivity amid life's inevitable changes. If negativity becomes overwhelming, seek counseling to transform unhealthy thought patterns. With concerted effort, we can move from pessimism's darkness into the illuminating light of optimism.

Chapter 2: Setting Intentions for Change

Clarifying Your Goals and Aspirations

The journey of self-improvement begins with a profound understanding of your deepest goals and aspirations. This introspective process allows you to align your objectives with your authentic self, creating a roadmap for meaningful growth. By taking the time to establish clarity of purpose, you can pursue holistic personal development across all facets of life.

The starting point involves reflection and enhanced self-awareness. Dedicate time for regular journaling, which enables you to methodically process thoughts, emotions, strengths and areas for improvement. The act of writing helps bring underlying desires and frustrations to the surface. Probing your experiences, core values and vision for the future lays the groundwork for aligned goals.

Once you achieve greater self-understanding, identifying your core values provides an anchor point. Assess what truly matters most, whether it be cultivating creativity, building relationships, pursuing professional ambitions, or living purposefully. Life priorities are highly personal, so take time for this assessment. Aligning goals with authentic values ensures a sense of fulfillment and passion.

With your values clarified, employ the SMART framework to formulate focused objectives. This involves setting goals that are Specific, Measurable, Achievable, Relevant and Time-bound. For example, rather than vaguely expressing you want to help people, set a goal to volunteer 10 hours per month at a local non-profit. Tangible goals are more readily achievable.

Since we have a tendency to take on too much, prioritizing goals is essential. The Eisenhower Matrix provides a useful method, categorizing tasks into four types: Urgent/Important, Important but not urgent, Urgent but not important, and Neither urgent nor important. This enables you to strategically focus energy where it matters most in both the short and long-term.

Supplement structured goal-setting with creative visualization techniques like vision boards or mental imagery. Compiling inspiring images, quotes and affirmations that symbolize your goals crystallizes them visually. Mentally picturing the realization of your goals also reinforces the motivation to achieve them.

While personal reflection is crucial, also seek out external perspectives. Discussing goals with a mentor or trusted friend solicits constructive feedback. Their objective insights help refine and clarify objectives. Different viewpoints illuminate blind spots we cannot see.

With well-defined goals, break them down into manageable action steps. Pursuing a large goal like starting a business is less overwhelming when you systematically break it down into smaller milestones. Completing each next step builds momentum.

Remember to build in regular reviews of your goals as part of the process. Life brings constant changes, so goals require reassessment. What energized you months ago may have shifted, and that is perfectly fine. Periodic evaluation ensures your goals continue resonating.

Cultivating a growth mindset is equally important, where you view challenges as opportunities for self-improvement rather than insurmountable obstacles. Maintaining positive perspective builds resilience when you inevitably face setbacks pursuing your aspirations.

Continuous learning is also pivotal. Identify knowledge and skills you will need to actualize your vision. Perhaps you want to build public speaking skills or learn website development. Lifelong learning is a journey unto itself that reinforces your goals.

The process of defining and refining your personal goals and aspirations takes introspection, self-honesty and regular reevaluation. But crafting objectives aligned with your authentic values is the compass that steers you down the path toward greater fulfillment. Your goals manifest your best vision of yourself and the world. Keep them at the forefront as guideposts directing your self-improvement.

Creating a Vision for Your Positive Future

Defining a clear, vivid vision of your desired future serves as a guiding North Star, illuminating the path toward self-transformation. This vision becomes the overarching goal influencing choices, fueling motivation during challenges, and providing clarity of purpose. A well-crafted future vision immerses you in the sights, sounds and emotions of your realized aspirations, propelling you forward.

Begin crafting your vision by focusing on continuous personal growth and development. Imagine acquiring new skills, knowledge and experiences that allow you to evolve into the best version of yourself. Include physical, mental and emotional aspects of health and wellness. Envision leading a balanced lifestyle that enriches your existence.

Define the meaningful connections and fulfilling relationships that contribute to a well-rounded life. Consider the positive impact you want to have on others through sincerity, compassion and wisdom. Articulate your professional ambitions and how your talents and passions will shape your career and contribution to society.

Visually immerse yourself in the lifestyle and environment that nurtures your version of success. Picture your daily habits, community, and living conditions. Clearly outline the value system guiding your behaviors and choices. Your vision should resonate with your authentic self.

Employ practical techniques to make this vision tangible. Spend time vividly imagining how your positive future will look, sound and feel. Compile vision boards with meaningful images, quotes and objects representing your aspirations. Articulate your vision in a journal, capturing nuances and emotions. Set aligned interim goals as stepping stones.

Revisit and refine this vision periodically as you evolve. Use affirmations and optimistic language to reinforce it. Repeatedly immerse yourself in this envisioned future until it feels abundantly real and within reach. Let it inspire clarity within your deepest motivations and purpose.

Integrate this vision into your daily life as a guiding framework. Begin each morning by reconnecting to your aspirations. Incorporate it into rituals to set an intentional tone for the day. When faced with choices, evaluate whether they align with your positive future vision. Develop ways to track your progress, celebrating each achievement.

By defining and constantly revisiting a detailed vision of your best life, you plant the seeds that will blossom into reality. This clarity of purpose focuses your present. When you vividly imagine your future self, you become increasingly motivated to mirror that vision in daily life.

Keep this vision alive by engaging all your senses. When challenges arise, retreat into it for renewed clarity and strength. It represents the realization of your life's purpose. With consistent mindset shifts and aligned actions, you narrow the gap between present and future, bringing your boldest dreams into focus.

Chapter 3: Mindfulness and Self-Awareness

Practicing Mindful Living

The essence of mindful living lies in the art of being fully present and engaged in each moment as it unfolds, rather than dwelling in memories of the past or anticipating the future. This way of being provides a unique vantage point from which we can navigate life's complexities with enhanced clarity, equanimity and intentionality. Mindful living serves as a guiding light, fostering emotional balance, alleviating stress, sharpening focus and ultimately leading to a richer experience of daily existence.

Mindful living encourages us to embrace the beauty and possibilities of the present moment. When we train our minds to inhabit the here and now rather than being trapped in automatic thoughts and habits, we create space to connect more deeply with both ourselves and the world around us. This presence becomes a transformative force, infusing our actions with heightened awareness and our experiences with a sense of appreciation and wonder.

One of the gifts of practicing mindfulness is an increased capacity for emotional regulation. By impartially observing our emotions as they arise without immediately reacting or judging, we can respond more thoughtfully in the moment rather than being driven by impulsive reactions. This emotional intelligence becomes a powerful tool in navigating complex relationships and challenges, providing a foundation of resilience even in the face of adversity.

Mindful living also acts as a balm that soothes our nervous systems and provides respite from the relentless stresses of modern life. The practice of continually redirecting our focus to the present reality rather than getting entangled in worries about the uncertain future or regrets about the unchangeable past alleviates much of the mental burden that accompanies anxiety and rumination. This shift in perspective cultivates an oasis of calm and tranquility amid life's turbulence.

Additionally, the practice of present-moment mindfulness trains our minds to remain anchored and concentrated regardless of distractions, thereby nurturing enhanced cognitive skills. Just as repetitive physical exercise strengthens the body, regular meditation enhances mental endurance, focus and working memory capacity. This improved concentration and acuity contributes to increased productivity, learning and engagement with each moment.

The journey of mindful living is also a journey inward, providing a map to greater self-understanding. By impartially observing our moment-to-moment thoughts, beliefs, emotional states and behavioral tendencies, we can gain penetrating insight into the dynamics of our inner worlds. This heightened self-awareness becomes the bedrock on which we can build enduring personal growth and development.

Several philosophical principles illuminate the pathway to a mindful life and provide guidance on how to weave this practice into the fabric of daily living:

Cultivating a non-judgmental witnessing of each experience invites us to observe thoughts and emotions with curiosity rather than labeling them as good or bad. This builds acceptance and discernment. Approaching each moment with a beginner's mind opens us to novelty, wonder and being fully engaged rather than acting on autopilot. Radical acceptance of the present moment, without needing to control or fundamentally change it, fosters tranquility amid life's ups and downs. Anchoring attention on the breath nourishes awareness of the present. Expressing gratitude redirects focus away from perceived lack toward appreciation of blessings.

There are many practical methods for cultivating mindful living. Setting aside time for formal daily meditation establishes a powerful ritual for training the mind and sustaining presence throughout each day. Integrating mindful movement practices like yoga, qigong or walking meditation harmonizes physical activity with enhanced awareness. Conscious eating involves savoring each bite while tuning into the sensual pleasures and nourishment of a meal. Unplugging from digital devices temporarily creates space for us to reconnect with ourselves and our surroundings. Maintaining a daily gratitude journal recalibrates the mind toward life's abundance. Listening fully and speaking mindfully cultivates authentic presence and understanding in all interactions.

We can additionally integrate mindfulness into the fabric of daily living through centering morning rituals, pausing mindfully during transitions between activities, frequent check-ins to monitor our inner landscape, and reflecting each evening on moments of mindfulness that day. By fully inhabiting each moment with all our senses and maintaining heart-centered awareness, we reduce anxiety about the future while deriving profound meaning and joy from ordinary human experiences. Mindfulness is both a practice and a way of being that illuminates our lives from the inside out. The essence of mindful living lies in the art of being fully present and engaged in each moment as it unfolds, rather than dwelling in memories of the past or anticipating the future. This way of being provides a unique vantage point from which we can navigate life's complexities with enhanced clarity, equanimity and intentionality. Mindful living serves as a guiding light, fostering emotional balance, alleviating stress, sharpening focus and ultimately leading to a richer experience of daily existence.

Mindful living encourages us to embrace the beauty and possibilities of the present moment. When we train our minds to inhabit the here and now rather than being trapped in automatic thoughts and habits, we create space to connect more deeply with both ourselves and the world around us. This presence becomes a transformative force, infusing our actions with heightened awareness and our experiences with a sense of appreciation and wonder.

One of the gifts of practicing mindfulness is an increased capacity for emotional regulation. By impartially observing our emotions as they arise without immediately reacting or judging, we can respond more thoughtfully in the moment rather than being driven by impulsive reactions. This emotional intelligence becomes a powerful tool in navigating complex relationships and challenges, providing a foundation of resilience even in the face of adversity.

Mindful living also acts as a balm that soothes our nervous systems and provides respite from the relentless stresses of modern life. The practice of continually redirecting our focus to the present reality rather than getting entangled in worries about the uncertain future or regrets about the unchangeable past alleviates much of the mental burden that accompanies anxiety and rumination. This shift in perspective cultivates an oasis of calm and tranquility amid life's turbulence.

Additionally, the practice of present-moment mindfulness trains our minds to remain anchored and concentrated regardless of distractions, thereby nurturing enhanced cognitive skills. Just as repetitive physical exercise strengthens the body, regular meditation enhances mental endurance, focus and working memory capacity. This improved concentration and acuity contributes to increased productivity, learning and engagement with each moment.

The journey of mindful living is also a journey inward, providing a map to greater self-understanding. By impartially observing our moment-to-moment thoughts, beliefs, emotional states and behavioral tendencies, we can gain penetrating insight into the dynamics of our inner worlds. This heightened self-awareness becomes the bedrock on which we can build enduring personal growth and development.

Several philosophical principles illuminate the pathway to a mindful life and provide guidance on how to weave this practice into the fabric of daily living:

Cultivating a non-judgmental witnessing of each experience invites us to observe thoughts and emotions with curiosity rather than labeling them as good or bad. This builds acceptance and discernment. Approaching each moment with a beginner's mind opens us to novelty, wonder and being fully engaged rather than acting on autopilot. Radical acceptance of the present moment, without needing to control or fundamentally change it, fosters tranquility amid life's ups and downs. Anchoring attention on the breath nourishes awareness of the present. Expressing gratitude redirects focus away from perceived lack toward appreciation of blessings.

There are many practical methods for cultivating mindful living. Setting aside time for formal daily meditation establishes a powerful ritual for training the mind and sustaining presence throughout each day. Integrating mindful movement practices like yoga, qigong or walking meditation harmonizes physical activity with enhanced awareness. Conscious eating involves savoring each bite while tuning into the sensual pleasures and nourishment of a meal. Unplugging from digital devices temporarily creates space for us to reconnect with ourselves and our surroundings. Maintaining a daily gratitude journal recalibrates the mind toward life's abundance. Listening fully and speaking mindfully cultivates authentic presence and understanding in all interactions.

We can additionally integrate mindfulness into the fabric of daily living through centering morning rituals, pausing mindfully during transitions between activities, frequent check-ins to monitor our inner landscape, and reflecting each evening on moments of mindfulness that day. By fully inhabiting each moment with all our senses and maintaining heart-centered awareness, we reduce anxiety about the future while deriving profound meaning and joy from ordinary human experiences. Mindfulness is both a practice and a way of being that illuminates our lives from the inside out.

Developing Self-Awareness for Personal Growth

Self-awareness is the essential foundation for meaningful and sustainable personal growth. By cultivating a deeper understanding of our inner landscape - our thoughts, beliefs, emotional patterns, strengths and weaknesses - we establish a solid basis from which to foster positive change.

Enhancing self-awareness begins with carving out time for regular self-reflection through journaling, meditation and mindfulness. Setting the intention to honestly observe our mental and emotional worlds without judgement allows insights to organically emerge. We may uncover recurring destructive thought patterns like pessimism or core limiting beliefs rooted in past experiences. Bringing these into conscious awareness is the first step toward transformation.

Seeking feedback from trusted friends and mentors can also shed light on blind spots we are unable to see. Others often notice self-sabotaging habits, defenses, or communication barriers we have. Receiving this constructive input with openness and applying it facilitates growth. We all have areas for improvement if we have the courage to ask.

It is also important to identify our innate strengths, values and passions. Self-awareness is not solely about recognizing flaws but also honoring our gifts and inner wisdom. Reflect on the unique talents you possess, the core values that provide an inner compass and the types of activities that ignite your spirit. Knowing our light is as crucial as knowing our darkness.

As self-awareness deepens, pay close attention to how you respond in difficult situations and challenging relationships. Do you tend to lash out in anger? Shut down emotionally? The instinctive ways we react reveal much about our triggers and emotional blocks. Learning to catch ourselves in old patterns is liberating.

Notice the stories you perpetually tell yourself about who you are and what you are capable of. Do you cling to old labels and underestimate your abilities? Strategic self-talk shapes our self-image. Becoming aware of limiting self-narratives allows us to intentionally cultivate empowering ones aligned with our highest potential.

There are a few key pitfalls to avoid on the path of self-awareness. Be wary of getting stuck in excessive rumination without positive action. The goal is active self-improvement, not just passive naval-gazing. Also avoid making harsh self-judgments in the process. The more we embrace self-awareness with compassion, the more we will thrive.

Ultimately, self-knowledge is only worthwhile if put into practice. Use what you learn about yourself to make intentional changes, both inward and outward. For example, if you discover a tendency to focus on the negative, make adjustments to consciously reframe your thinking and limit consuming overly cynical media. If you struggle to express vulnerability, determine small ways to open up with loved ones. Set progressive goals and celebrate small wins.

The quest for self-awareness requires brutal honesty, consistent self-inquiry, and the willingness to step outside comfort zones. But few endeavors are more vital for expanding our horizons and creating lives of deeper purpose and joy. As we come to know ourselves inside and out, we gain power over inner demons, align with our highest ideals and become architects of our destiny. We move from unconscious living to sculpting our life by conscious design.

So take time to retreat inwards through whatever self-reflective practices resonate, whether meditation, creative expression or periods of solitude in nature. There is no limit to self-awareness if we devote ourselves to the discipline of understanding the terrain of our inner world. Therein lies the wellspring of resilience required to endure life's trials and the wisdom that frees our minds. Know thyself, and you shall be empowered to grow, transform and contribute in ways that uplift us all.Here is a 1027 word extensive discussion on developing self-awareness for personal growth:

Self-awareness is the essential foundation for meaningful and sustainable personal growth. By cultivating a deeper understanding of our inner landscape - our thoughts, beliefs, emotional patterns, strengths and weaknesses - we establish a solid basis from which to foster positive change.

Enhancing self-awareness begins with carving out time for regular self-reflection through journaling, meditation and mindfulness. Setting the intention to honestly observe our mental and emotional worlds without judgement allows insights to organically emerge. We may uncover recurring destructive thought patterns like pessimism or core limiting beliefs rooted in past experiences. Bringing these into conscious awareness is the first step toward transformation.

Seeking feedback from trusted friends and mentors can also shed light on blind spots we are unable to see. Others often notice self-sabotaging habits, defenses, or communication barriers we have. Receiving this constructive input with openness and applying it facilitates growth. We all have areas for improvement if we have the courage to ask.

It is also important to identify our innate strengths, values and passions. Self-awareness is not solely about recognizing flaws but also honoring our gifts and inner wisdom. Reflect on the unique talents you possess, the core values that provide an inner compass and the types of activities that ignite your spirit. Knowing our light is as crucial as knowing our darkness.

As self-awareness deepens, pay close attention to how you respond in difficult situations and challenging relationships. Do you tend to lash out in anger? Shut down emotionally? The instinctive ways we react reveal much about our triggers and emotional blocks. Learning to catch ourselves in old patterns is liberating.

Notice the stories you perpetually tell yourself about who you are and what you are capable of. Do you cling to old labels and underestimate your abilities? Strategic self-talk shapes our self-image. Becoming aware of limiting self-narratives allows us to intentionally cultivate empowering ones aligned with our highest potential.

There are a few key pitfalls to avoid on the path of self-awareness. Be wary of getting stuck in excessive rumination without positive action. The goal is active self-improvement, not just passive naval-gazing. Also avoid making harsh self-judgments in the process. The more we embrace self-awareness with compassion, the more we will thrive.

Ultimately, self-knowledge is only worthwhile if put into practice. Use what you learn about yourself to make intentional changes, both inward and outward. For example, if you discover a tendency to focus on the negative, make adjustments to consciously reframe your thinking and limit consuming overly cynical media. If you struggle to express vulnerability, determine small ways to open up with loved ones. Set progressive goals and celebrate small wins.

The quest for self-awareness requires brutal honesty, consistent self-inquiry, and the willingness to step outside comfort zones. But few endeavors are more vital for expanding our horizons and creating lives of deeper purpose and joy. As we come to know ourselves inside and out, we gain power over inner demons, align with our highest ideals and become architects of our destiny. We move from unconscious living to sculpting our life by conscious design.

So take time to retreat inwards through whatever self-reflective practices resonate, whether meditation, creative expression or periods of solitude in nature. There is no limit to self-awareness if we devote ourselves to the discipline of understanding the terrain of our inner world. Therein lies the wellspring of resilience required to endure life's trials and the wisdom that frees our minds. Know thyself, and you shall be empowered to grow, transform and contribute in ways that uplift us all.

Chapter 4: Nurturing Healthy Habits

Establishing Positive Daily Routines

Implementing positive daily routines is a fundamental strategy for achieving goals, boosting productivity, managing stress and enriching wellbeing. Life's demands can seem overwhelming, but constructive rituals provide structure, focus and a sense of purpose to each day. With intention and consistency, we can optimize mornings, workflow, health habits and evenings through beneficial routines.

An energizing morning routine is the foundation for a productive day. Waking up earlier creates spaciousness for centering rituals. Begin with mindfulness practices like meditating, journaling or sipping tea while looking out the window. Exercise first thing to circulate energy. Eat a nutritious breakfast to fuel the body and mind. Avoid screens for the first hour to retain mental clarity. Establishing an intentional morning routine minimizes chaos and sets the tone.

Similarly, incorporating purposeful breaks between tasks enhances productivity and wellbeing. Our minds require regular rest from concentrated effort to replenish focus and creativity. Schedule short breaks for light exercise, chatting with a colleague, listening to music or doing mini-meditations. The brain is rejuvenated when we intersperse effort with rest. Protect downtime in routines.

Another element is scheduling higher concentration work during peak energy times when possible. For example, if mornings are when you feel sharpest, prioritize more complex projects then. Know your body's rhythms and align key tasks with optimal timing. Also be sure to take a real lunch break, getting away from your desk.Honoring natural patterns of energy keeps you firing on all cylinders.

In addition, interspersing lighter and heavier tasks promotes sustained efficiency while adding diversity. Balance meetings and email catch-up with periods for thoughtful project work. Vary sitting tasks with moving ones. Switch between analytical and creative modes. Blend collaborative and solo work. Routines feel less monotonous when we sprinkle in this variety.

Building regular exercise into each day also pays dividends for both physical and mental health. It could be a gym session, walk outside, yoga class or home strength routine. Make it easy and enticing to stay consistent. Pair it with a rewarding podcast or music playlist. Adding activity to daily rituals makes you feel rejuvenated.

Likewise, scheduling time for meal planning and preparation helps maintain healthy eating habits long-term. Devote part of a weekend day to grocery shop, prep batch meals for the week and reorganize the kitchen. Refueling with nutritious whole foods sustains energy and immunity. Make eating well effortless through routines.

In addition, establish technology and screen time limits to prevent burnout. For example, turn off email notifications after a certain hour and put away phones during meals. Set time restrictions on distracting apps. Unplug completely before bed. Adding boundaries creates space for recharging.

Finally, nightly wind-down rituals set you up for high-quality sleep. Develop routines like taking a warm bath, reading fiction, trying a gentle yoga sequence, dimming lights and avoiding electronics before bed. Consistent sleep hygiene reduces insomnia and makes mornings easier. Let go of the day.

Breaking Unhealthy Patterns

Understanding Unhealthy Patterns:

Unhealthy patterns manifest in various aspects of our lives, ranging from destructive thought patterns and self-sabotaging behaviors to ingrained habits that compromise our physical and mental well-being. These patterns often stem from a combination of past experiences, learned behaviors, and deeply rooted beliefs. To embark on the journey of breaking unhealthy patterns, it is essential to first understand their origin and the role they play in our lives.

Psychological Roots:

Unhealthy patterns frequently find their roots in psychological mechanisms such as cognitive biases, defense mechanisms, and conditioned responses. These mechanisms, shaped by past experiences and environmental influences, create automatic reactions that contribute to the perpetuation of unhealthy patterns.

Emotional Impact:

The emotional dimension of unhealthy patterns is profound. Patterns often serve as coping mechanisms, providing a sense of familiarity and control in the face of stress, anxiety, or unresolved emotions. Breaking these patterns requires a deep exploration of the underlying emotions and a willingness to confront discomfort.

Behavioral Manifestations:

Whether it's the repetitive cycle of destructive relationships, self-sabotaging behaviors, or addictive tendencies, unhealthy patterns manifest behaviorally. Breaking these patterns involves unraveling the behavioral aspects and implementing intentional changes in daily actions and responses.

The Complexity of Breaking Unhealthy Patterns:

The process of breaking unhealthy patterns is far from linear; it is marked by complexity, challenges, and moments of profound self-discovery. Critical examination of this process unveils the multifaceted nature of personal transformation.

1. Self-Awareness:

Central to breaking unhealthy patterns is cultivating self-awareness. This involves a deep and honest introspection to recognize the patterns that hinder growth. The journey of self-awareness is a continuous process, requiring the courage to confront uncomfortable truths about oneself.

2. Identification of Triggers:

Unhealthy patterns often have triggers—specific situations, emotions, or stressors that activate them. Identifying these triggers is crucial in understanding the patterns' dynamics and implementing proactive strategies to navigate them more effectively.

3. Mindfulness and Reflection:

Mindfulness becomes a powerful ally in breaking unhealthy patterns. By bringing conscious awareness to the present moment, individuals gain the capacity to observe patterns as they emerge. Reflection, whether through journaling or therapeutic conversations, allows for a deeper understanding of the thought processes and behaviors entwined in these patterns.

4. Challenging Cognitive Distortions:

Unhealthy patterns often involve distorted thinking patterns or irrational beliefs. Challenging these cognitive distortions is a critical step in reshaping thought processes. Cognitive-behavioral interventions and therapeutic approaches provide tools to reframe negative thought patterns.

5. Behavioral Modification:

Transformation requires intentional behavioral modification. This involves replacing unhealthy behaviors with healthier alternatives. It might entail building new habits, adopting coping mechanisms, or restructuring daily routines to foster positive change.

6. Emotional Regulation:

Emotional intelligence is foundational in breaking unhealthy patterns. Learning to navigate and regulate emotions diminishes the reliance on maladaptive patterns as coping mechanisms. This process involves developing a more constructive relationship with emotions and seeking healthy outlets for expression.

7. Support Systems and Accountability:

The journey of breaking unhealthy patterns benefits from a supportive environment. Engaging with a therapist, joining support groups, or confiding in trusted friends creates a network of accountability. These external supports offer guidance, encouragement, and perspectives that contribute to sustained change.

The Role of Therapy in Breaking Unhealthy Patterns:

Therapeutic interventions play a pivotal role in the process of breaking unhealthy patterns. Therapists serve as guides, providing a structured space for exploration, introspection, and skill-building. Various therapeutic modalities, including cognitive-behavioral therapy, dialectical behavior therapy, and psychodynamic approaches, offer tailored strategies for breaking patterns based on individual needs.

1. Cognitive-Behavioral Therapy (CBT):

CBT is particularly effective in addressing unhealthy thought patterns and behaviors. Through collaborative efforts between the therapist and the individual, CBT identifies and challenges distorted thinking, fostering cognitive restructuring and behavior modification.

2. Dialectical Behavior Therapy (DBT):

DBT, originally developed to treat borderline personality disorder, is valuable in addressing patterns of emotional dysregulation and self-destructive behaviors. It emphasizes skills training in mindfulness, distress tolerance, emotion regulation, and interpersonal effectiveness.

3. Psychodynamic Approaches:

Psychodynamic therapy explores the deeper roots of unhealthy patterns, delving into unconscious processes and unresolved conflicts. By bringing unconscious material to consciousness, individuals gain insights that contribute to lasting change.

Challenges and Resilience in Breaking Unhealthy Patterns:

The journey of breaking unhealthy patterns is not without its challenges. It requires resilience, commitment, and an acknowledgment that setbacks are inherent to the process. Critical examination of these challenges unveils the nuances of personal growth.

1. Fear of Change:

The fear of the unknown and the discomfort associated with change can impede progress. Acknowledging this fear and reframing it as a natural part of growth is essential in overcoming the resistance to change.

2. Relapse and Setbacks:

Relapse and setbacks are common in the process of breaking unhealthy patterns. Understanding that setbacks do not equate to failure but rather present opportunities for learning and refinement is crucial in maintaining resilience.

3. Identity and Self-Image:

Unhealthy patterns often become intertwined with one's identity. Breaking these patterns may challenge existing notions of self. Embracing the evolution of identity as a dynamic process allows for greater adaptability and growth.

4. Long-Term Commitment:

Sustainable change requires a long-term commitment. Individuals may encounter moments of fatigue or disillusionment. Maintaining motivation involves periodically revisiting the reasons for embarking on the journey and celebrating incremental victories.

Chapter 5: Building Resilience

Embracing Challenges as Opportunities

Understanding Challenges as Inevitable and Intrinsic:

Challenges are an intrinsic aspect of the human journey, arising from the dynamic interplay of external circumstances and internal responses. They manifest in various forms — from personal setbacks and professional hurdles to unforeseen life events. Recognizing challenges as inevitable and inherent reframes their role from mere obstacles to integral components of the human experience.

1. Normalizing Adversity:

Embracing challenges begins with normalizing the concept of adversity. Rather than viewing challenges as anomalies to be avoided, adopting a perspective that acknowledges their inevitability fosters a mindset shift. This shift lays the foundation for cultivating resilience and adaptability.

2. Opportunities for Growth:

Challenges, when approached with the right mindset, become catalysts for personal and professional growth. Each obstacle presents an opportunity to learn, adapt, and develop new skills. The transformative power of challenges lies in their capacity to propel individuals beyond their comfort zones, fostering continuous evolution.

3. Navigating Uncertainty:

Life is inherently uncertain, and challenges often emerge in moments of unpredictability. Embracing challenges involves cultivating the resilience to navigate uncertainty with a sense of curiosity and openness. This mindset reframes uncertainty as a canvas for potential rather than a source of fear.

4. Building Resilience:

Resilience, the ability to bounce back from adversity, is a cornerstone of embracing challenges. Rather than viewing setbacks as insurmountable obstacles, individuals with a resilient mindset approach them as opportunities to strengthen their adaptive capacities. Resilience becomes a skill honed through the process of facing and overcoming challenges.

Psychological Dimensions of Embracing Challenges:

The psychological underpinnings of embracing challenges delve into cognitive processes, emotional responses, and the intricate ways in which individuals interpret and navigate the adversities they encounter.

1. Cognitive Reframing:

The cognitive aspect of embracing challenges involves reframing negative thought patterns. Instead of perceiving challenges through a lens of defeat, individuals can reframe them as opportunities for learning and development. Cognitive reframing empowers individuals to approach challenges with a growth-oriented mindset.

2. Mindset Shift:

Carol Dweck's concept of a growth mindset highlights the importance of perceiving challenges as opportunities for growth. A growth mindset views abilities as malleable and intelligence as something that can be developed over time. Embracing challenges with a growth mindset transforms setbacks into stepping stones toward improvement.

3. Adaptive Coping Strategies:

The psychological response to challenges often involves coping strategies. Embracing challenges requires the cultivation of adaptive coping mechanisms that enable individuals to manage stress, regulate emotions, and maintain a sense of efficacy in the face of adversity. These strategies contribute to psychological well-being.

4. Self-Efficacy and Confidence:

Overcoming challenges enhances self-efficacy — the belief in one's ability to achieve goals and overcome difficulties. As individuals successfully navigate challenges, their confidence in their capabilities grows. This positive reinforcement becomes a psychological resource that empowers them to tackle future challenges.

Emotional Dimensions:

Embracing challenges involves navigating a spectrum of emotions, from initial discomfort and frustration to the eventual sense of accomplishment. Understanding the emotional dimensions provides insight into the intricate interplay between challenges and emotional well-being.

1. Acceptance of Discomfort:

Challenges often elicit discomfort, and embracing them requires an acceptance of this initial unease. The ability to sit with discomfort without being overwhelmed allows individuals to move through the emotional spectrum and opens the door to transformative experiences.

2. Frustration as Motivation:

Rather than viewing frustration as a roadblock, embracing challenges involves transforming it into a motivational force. Frustration can be a catalyst for innovation, creativity, and the determination to find alternative solutions. It becomes a driving force that propels individuals forward.

3. Sense of Accomplishment:

Successfully navigating challenges brings about a profound sense of accomplishment. This emotional reward reinforces the idea that challenges are not merely obstacles but opportunities for personal triumph. The positive emotions associated with accomplishment contribute to overall well-being.

4. Cultivating Emotional Agility:

Emotional agility, the ability to navigate one's emotions with flexibility and resilience, plays a pivotal role in embracing challenges. Cultivating emotional agility involves recognizing and accepting emotions without judgment, allowing individuals to respond adaptively to challenges.

Behavioral Dimensions:

Behavioral responses to challenges encompass actions, problem-solving strategies, and the ways individuals engage with the external world. Examining these dimensions provides insights into the tangible actions that characterize a mindset of embracing challenges.

1. Proactive Problem-Solving:

Embracing challenges involves a proactive approach to problem-solving. Rather than passively reacting to difficulties, individuals with this mindset actively seek solutions, explore alternatives, and view setbacks as opportunities to refine their approach.

2. Adaptability and Flexibility:

Behavioral adaptability and flexibility are key components of embracing challenges. This involves adjusting one's strategies, re-evaluating goals, and being open to change when faced with obstacles. A flexible approach allows for a more dynamic and effective response to challenges.

3. Learning Orientation:

Individuals who embrace challenges exhibit a learning orientation — a commitment to extracting lessons from every experience. This behavioral aspect involves a continuous cycle of feedback, reflection, and adjustment based on the insights gained from navigating challenges.

4. Initiative and Agency:

Embracing challenges requires a sense of initiative and agency — the belief that individuals have the power to influence outcomes. Taking proactive steps, assuming responsibility for one's actions, and maintaining a sense of agency contribute to a constructive engagement with challenges.

Cultivating a Culture of Challenge Embrace:

The concept of embracing challenges extends beyond individual attitudes to encompass organizational and societal perspectives. Fostering a culture that values challenges as opportunities creates an environment conducive to innovation, growth, and collective well-being.

1. Organizational Innovation:

In organizational settings, a culture that embraces challenges fosters innovation. Rather than fearing failure, employees are encouraged to take calculated risks, experiment with new ideas, and view setbacks as valuable feedback. This culture of innovation propels organizations toward continuous improvement.

2. Educational Paradigm:

Within the realm of education, embracing challenges transforms the learning paradigm. Educational institutions that promote a growth mindset cultivate students' resilience, curiosity, and adaptability. Challenges become integral to the learning process, preparing students for real-world complexities.

3. Community Resilience:

At the societal level, communities that embrace challenges develop resilience. Whether facing economic uncertainties, environmental changes, or social shifts, communities that view challenges as opportunities for collective growth exhibit a heightened ability to adapt and thrive.

Strengthening Your Mental Resilience

Understanding Mental Resilience:

Mental resilience is not a static trait but a dynamic process that involves the cultivation of adaptive responses to life's inevitable ups and downs. It goes beyond mere coping and encompasses the capacity to grow and thrive in the face of adversity. Understanding the nuances of mental resilience requires an exploration of its various dimensions.

1. Psychological Flexibility:

At the core of mental resilience lies psychological flexibility — the ability to adapt and adjust one's cognitive processes to different situations. Individuals with high psychological flexibility can reframe challenges, regulate emotions, and maintain a balanced perspective in the midst of adversity.

2. Coping Strategies:

Effective coping strategies are pivotal in building mental resilience. These strategies encompass a range of approaches, from problem-solving and seeking social support to practicing mindfulness and engaging in activities that promote emotional well-being. The diversity of coping strategies allows individuals to tailor their responses to specific stressors.

3. Optimism and Positive Thinking:

A positive outlook and optimism contribute significantly to mental resilience. Cultivating a mindset that focuses on possibilities, acknowledges strengths, and fosters positive thinking enhances the ability to navigate challenges with resilience. Optimism serves as a buffer against the negative impact of stressors.

4. Self-Efficacy and Confidence:

Believing in one's ability to overcome challenges is a key component of mental resilience. Self-efficacy, the confidence in one's capabilities, empowers individuals to face difficulties with a sense of agency. This belief in one's capacity to influence outcomes is foundational to bouncing back from setbacks.

Psychological Dimensions of Mental Resilience:

The psychological dimensions of mental resilience delve into cognitive processes, emotional regulation, and the ways individuals interpret and respond to adversity.

1. Cognitive Appraisal:

How individuals appraise and interpret stressors influences their level of mental resilience. A resilient mindset involves viewing challenges as opportunities for growth, reframing setbacks as temporary, and maintaining a sense of control over one's responses.

2. Adaptive Thinking:

Mental resilience is closely tied to adaptive thinking patterns. The ability to adapt one's thoughts to align with reality, challenge negative beliefs, and engage in constructive self-talk fosters resilience. Cognitive restructuring techniques, often employed in cognitive-behavioral therapy, contribute to the development of adaptive thinking.

3. Emotional Regulation:

Emotional resilience is a significant aspect of mental resilience. The capacity to identify, understand, and regulate emotions allows individuals to navigate stressors without being overwhelmed. Emotional regulation strategies, such as mindfulness and relaxation techniques, play a crucial role in this dimension.

4. Post-Traumatic Growth:

An advanced dimension of mental resilience is post-traumatic growth — the positive psychological changes that individuals experience as a result of coping with and overcoming adversity. This transformative process involves finding new perspectives, developing a deeper sense of meaning, and discovering personal strengths in the aftermath of trauma.

Emotional Dimensions:

Emotional dimensions of mental resilience encompass how individuals experience and manage emotions in response to stressors.

1. Resilience to Negative Emotions:

Mental resilience involves the ability to bounce back from negative emotions. Rather than being overwhelmed by sadness, anxiety, or frustration, resilient individuals can acknowledge and process these emotions, allowing them to move through challenging experiences with emotional agility.

2. Positive Emotional Outlook:

Maintaining a positive emotional outlook, even in the face of adversity, characterizes mental resilience. This outlook involves cultivating positive emotions such as gratitude, joy, and hope. Positive emotions serve as resources that counterbalance the impact of stressors.

3. Flexibility in Emotional Responses:

Flexibility in emotional responses is integral to mental resilience. Instead of being rigid in emotional reactions, resilient individuals can adapt their emotional responses to different situations. This flexibility allows for a more adaptive and nuanced approach to challenges.

4. Embracing Discomfort:

Mental resilience entails an acceptance of discomfort. Resilient individuals can sit with uncomfortable emotions without being consumed by them. This ability to tolerate emotional discomfort contributes to a greater sense of emotional resilience.

Behavioral Dimensions:

Behavioral dimensions of mental resilience encompass the actions, habits, and choices individuals make in response to stressors.

1. Proactive Problem-Solving:

Proactively addressing challenges through effective problem-solving is a behavioral aspect of mental resilience. Resilient individuals take initiative, assess the situation, and actively seek solutions rather than passively reacting to difficulties.

2. Healthy Lifestyle Choices:

Engaging in behaviors that promote overall well-being contributes to mental resilience. This includes adopting a healthy lifestyle through regular exercise, balanced nutrition, sufficient sleep, and avoiding maladaptive coping mechanisms such as substance abuse.

3. Seeking Social Support:

Building and maintaining a support network is a behavioral strategy that enhances mental resilience. Seeking social support during times of stress fosters connection, provides a sense of belonging, and offers practical assistance in navigating challenges.

4. Adaptability in Behavior:

Behavioral adaptability involves adjusting one's actions in response to changing circumstances. Resilient individuals can modify their behavior, reassess goals, and pivot when necessary, demonstrating a capacity to adapt to evolving challenges.

Cultivating Mental Resilience:

Cultivating mental resilience is an ongoing and intentional process that involves the development of cognitive, emotional, and behavioral skills. Strategies for building and strengthening mental resilience include:

1. Mindfulness and Meditation:

Practicing mindfulness and meditation cultivates present-moment awareness and emotional regulation. These practices enhance the ability to respond to stressors with a clear and focused mind.

2. Cognitive-Behavioral Therapy (CBT):

CBT is an evidence-based therapeutic approach that addresses maladaptive thought patterns and behaviors. It equips individuals with tools to reframe negative thinking, build coping skills, and enhance resilience.

3. Positive Psychology Interventions:

Positive psychology interventions focus on cultivating positive emotions, strengths, and a sense of meaning. Activities such as gratitude journaling, savoring positive experiences, and identifying personal strengths contribute to mental resilience.

4. Stress Inoculation Training:

Stress inoculation training involves gradually exposing individuals to stressors in a controlled setting. This technique helps build resilience by allowing individuals to develop effective coping strategies in a supportive environment.

Chapter 6: Cultivating Positive Relationships

Fostering Healthy Connections

Understanding Healthy Connections:

Healthy connections encompass a spectrum of relationships, including family bonds, friendships, romantic partnerships, and social connections. At the core of these connections is a sense of mutual support, understanding, and positive influence. Understanding the dynamics that contribute to healthy connections is essential for individuals seeking to enhance their overall well-being.

1. Mutual Respect and Understanding:

Healthy connections thrive on mutual respect and understanding. Individuals in these relationships acknowledge each other's perspectives, validate feelings, and engage in open and empathetic communication. This foundation creates a supportive environment where individuals feel heard and valued.

2. Trust and Reliability:

Trust is a cornerstone of healthy connections. Building and maintaining trust involves being reliable, keeping commitments, and demonstrating integrity. Trust fosters a sense of security in relationships, allowing individuals to be vulnerable and authentic with one another.

3. Positive Influence and Growth:

Healthy connections contribute to personal and mutual growth. Individuals in these relationships inspire and support each other's aspirations. The positive influence of healthy connections extends to emotional well-being, motivation, and the pursuit of shared or individual goals.

4. Effective Communication:

Communication is a key factor in healthy connections. Clear, honest, and open communication fosters understanding and prevents misunderstandings. Individuals in healthy relationships feel comfortable expressing their thoughts and emotions, contributing to a harmonious connection.

Psychological Benefits of Healthy Connections:

The impact of healthy connections on psychological well-being is profound, influencing emotional resilience, stress management, and overall mental health.

1. Emotional Support and Resilience:

Healthy connections provide a crucial source of emotional support. During challenging times, having someone to share burdens, offer comfort, and provide perspective enhances emotional resilience. Knowing that one is not alone in facing difficulties contributes to a positive psychological state.

2. Reduced Stress and Anxiety:

The presence of healthy connections has been linked to lower stress levels and reduced anxiety. The emotional support gained from these relationships acts as a buffer against the negative effects of stress, promoting a sense of security and calm.

3. Enhanced Self-Esteem:

Positive affirmations and encouragement from healthy connections contribute to enhanced self-esteem. Feeling valued and accepted by others fosters a positive self-image and a greater sense of self-worth.

4. Improved Emotional Regulation:

Interactions within healthy connections provide opportunities for emotional regulation. Whether through shared laughter, empathetic conversations, or collaborative problem-solving, these relationships contribute to emotional balance and well-being.

Emotional Dimensions of Healthy Connections:

The emotional dimensions of healthy connections delve into the various feelings and experiences individuals encounter within positive relationships.

1. Empathy and Compassion:

Healthy connections are characterized by empathy and compassion. Individuals in these relationships seek to understand each other's emotions, share in both joys and sorrows, and provide support without judgment.

2. Joy and Celebration:

Sharing moments of joy and celebration enhances the emotional connection between individuals. Whether celebrating personal achievements or collective milestones, these positive emotions strengthen the bond and create lasting memories.

3. Security and Comfort:

Feeling emotionally secure and comfortable in a connection is paramount. Healthy relationships provide a safe space where individuals can express vulnerabilities, share fears, and seek comfort without fear of judgment.

4. Fulfillment and Satisfaction:

Healthy connections contribute to emotional fulfillment and satisfaction. The positive emotional experiences gained from these relationships enrich one's overall sense of happiness and contentment.

Physical Benefits of Healthy Connections:

Beyond psychological and emotional well-being, healthy connections exert tangible effects on physical health and longevity.

1. Strengthened Immune System:

Studies suggest that individuals with strong social connections exhibit a strengthened immune system. The emotional support and positive influence of healthy connections contribute to overall health and resilience against illnesses.

2. Reduced Risk of Chronic Diseases:

Maintaining healthy connections has been linked to a reduced risk of chronic diseases. The stress-reducing effects of positive relationships positively impact cardiovascular health, immune function, and other physiological processes.

3. Longevity and Well-being:

Research consistently indicates a correlation between healthy connections and increased longevity. Individuals with a strong support system tend to lead healthier lifestyles, experience less chronic stress, and, as a result, enjoy a higher quality of life.

4. Quicker Recovery from Illness:

Individuals with robust social connections often experience quicker recovery from illness or surgery. The emotional and practical support provided by healthy connections contributes to a more efficient healing process.

Behavioral Dimensions of Healthy Connections:

The behavioral dimensions of healthy connections encompass the actions, habits, and choices that individuals make within the context of their relationships.

1. Reciprocity and Mutual Support:

Reciprocal actions and mutual support characterize healthy connections. Individuals actively engage in behaviors that contribute to the well-being of the relationship, fostering a sense of partnership and collaboration.

2. Shared Activities and Interests:

Participating in shared activities and interests strengthens healthy connections. Whether engaging in hobbies, exercise, or intellectual pursuits together, these shared experiences create bonds and deepen the connection.

3. Conflict Resolution and Communication:

Addressing conflicts through effective communication is a behavioral aspect of healthy connections. Individuals in these relationships prioritize resolving disagreements through open dialogue, compromise, and a commitment to understanding each other's perspectives.

4. Celebrating Milestones:

Behaviors that involve celebrating milestones and achievements contribute to the positive atmosphere of healthy connections. Recognizing and commemorating individual and shared accomplishments reinforces a sense of shared joy and accomplishment.

Cultivating and Sustaining Healthy Connections:

Cultivating and sustaining healthy connections is a dynamic and ongoing process that requires effort, communication, and mutual investment.

1. Effective Communication Skills:

Developing effective communication skills is fundamental to cultivating healthy connections. This includes active listening, expressing oneself clearly, and fostering an environment where individuals feel comfortable sharing their thoughts and feelings.

2. Boundaries and Respect:

Establishing and respecting boundaries is essential in healthy connections. Individuals should communicate their needs, expectations, and limits while respecting those of others. Clear boundaries contribute to a harmonious and respectful relationship.

3. Quality Time Together:

Spending quality time together is a cornerstone of healthy connections. Whether through shared meals, meaningful conversations, or engaging in activities, dedicating time to one another strengthens the bond and fosters connection.

4. Supportive and Positive Environment:

Creating a supportive and positive environment is vital for sustaining healthy connections. This involves offering encouragement, celebrating achievements, and providing comfort during challenging times.

Navigating Challenges in Relationships

Relationships are intricate and dynamic, often navigating through a myriad of challenges that test the strength and resilience of those involved. Whether in friendships, romantic partnerships, or familial connections, understanding how to navigate challenges is crucial for sustaining healthy and fulfilling relationships. In this comprehensive exploration, we delve into the complexities of relationship challenges, offering insights into common issues, effective communication strategies, and the transformative potential that arises from navigating obstacles together.

Understanding Common Relationship Challenges:

Communication Breakdown:

One of the most prevalent challenges in relationships is communication breakdown. Misunderstandings, unexpressed feelings, and differing communication styles can lead to conflicts and emotional distance.

Trust Issues:

Trust forms the foundation of any healthy relationship. Issues of trust can arise from past betrayals, secrecy, or unmet expectations, leading to a breakdown in the sense of security within the relationship.

Conflict and Disagreements:

Conflict is a natural part of any relationship, but unresolved disagreements can strain connections. Learning how to navigate conflicts constructively is essential for maintaining a healthy and thriving relationship.

Different Expectations:

Individuals in a relationship may have different expectations regarding various aspects, such as commitment, future plans, or even daily routines. Aligning these expectations is crucial for harmony.

Life Transitions and Stressors:

Life transitions, such as career changes, moving, or health issues, can introduce stressors that impact relationships. Adapting to these changes collectively can be challenging but is vital for relationship resilience.

Lack of Emotional Intimacy:

Emotional intimacy is the glue that binds individuals in a relationship. Challenges may arise when one or both partners feel emotionally distant or struggle to express vulnerability.

Effective Communication Strategies:

Active Listening:

Active listening involves fully concentrating, understanding, responding, and remembering what is being said. It promotes a deeper understanding of each other's perspectives.

Open and Honest Communication:

Creating a safe space for open and honest communication fosters trust and transparency. Encouraging vulnerability allows individuals to express their thoughts and feelings without fear of judgment.

Empathy and Understanding:

Cultivating empathy involves putting oneself in the other person's shoes, understanding their emotions, and validating their experiences. This fosters a sense of connection and mutual understanding.

Use of "I" Statements:

When addressing concerns or conflicts, using "I" statements instead of "you" statements can prevent blame and defensiveness. Expressing feelings from a personal perspective encourages constructive dialogue.

Clarifying Expectations:

To avoid misunderstandings, clarifying expectations is essential. Discussing and aligning expectations on various aspects of the relationship helps create a shared vision for the future.

Conflict Resolution Skills:

Developing effective conflict resolution skills involves staying calm, focusing on the issue at hand, and working collaboratively towards a solution. Avoiding blame and criticism contributes to a more constructive resolution.

Transformative Potential of Navigating Challenges Together:

Increased Resilience:

Successfully navigating challenges together enhances the resilience of the relationship. Shared experiences of overcoming obstacles create a sense of unity and strength.

Deeper Understanding:

Overcoming challenges requires a deep understanding of each other's values, motivations, and coping mechanisms. This increased understanding can lead to a more profound connection.

Individual and Collective Growth:

Navigating challenges often involves personal growth for each individual. Collectively, the couple or individuals within the relationship may grow stronger, more resilient, and more adaptable.

Rebuilding Trust:

Addressing trust issues and navigating through them can lead to the rebuilding of trust on a stronger foundation. Open communication and consistent actions contribute to rebuilding a sense of security.

Enhanced Problem-Solving Skills:

Successfully navigating challenges hones problem-solving skills within the relationship. Individuals become adept at collaborating, finding solutions, and adapting to new circumstances.

Improved Emotional Intimacy:

Facing challenges together fosters a sense of closeness and emotional intimacy. Sharing vulnerabilities and triumphs creates a deeper connection and reinforces the emotional bond.

Chapter 7: Self-Compassion and Gratitude

Developing a Compassionate Self-View

Developing a compassionate self-view is a transformative journey that involves cultivating understanding, kindness, and acceptance towards oneself. In a world that often emphasizes achievement and external validation, fostering self-compassion becomes a powerful tool for emotional well-being and personal growth. In this comprehensive exploration, we delve into the intricacies of developing a compassionate self-view, examining its psychological benefits, practical strategies, and the profound impact it can have on overall life satisfaction.

Understanding Self-Compassion:

Self-compassion is a concept rooted in mindfulness and self-kindness. It involves treating oneself with the same warmth and care that one would offer to a close friend in times of struggle or failure. Dr. Kristin Neff, a pioneering researcher in the field of self-compassion, identifies three core components:

Self-Kindness: Being understanding and gentle with oneself rather than harshly critical.

Common Humanity: Recognizing that personal struggles and imperfections are part of the shared human experience.

Mindfulness: Approaching one's experiences with a balanced and non-judgmental awareness.

Psychological Benefits of Developing Self-Compassion:

Increased Emotional Resilience:

Developing self-compassion enhances emotional resilience by providing a supportive internal environment. Individuals become better equipped to navigate challenges and setbacks with a sense of kindness and understanding.

Reduced Negative Self-Talk:

A compassionate self-view diminishes negative self-talk and self-criticism. Individuals learn to reframe their internal dialogue, fostering a more positive and nurturing relationship with themselves.

Improved Mental Health:

Self-compassion is linked to improved mental health outcomes. It correlates with lower levels of anxiety, depression, and stress, creating a buffer against the detrimental effects of negative emotions.

Enhanced Emotional Well-Being:

Embracing self-compassion contributes to enhanced emotional well-being. Individuals experience greater emotional balance, self-acceptance, and an overall positive outlook on life.

Greater Motivation and Goal Pursuit:

Contrary to the misconception that self-compassion may lead to complacency, research suggests that it fosters greater motivation and resilience in pursuing personal goals. Individuals are more likely to bounce back from setbacks and continue their efforts with self-encouragement.

Healthier Relationships:

Developing a compassionate self-view spills over into interpersonal relationships. Individuals who treat themselves with kindness are more likely to extend that compassion to others, fostering healthier and more fulfilling connections.

Practical Strategies for Developing Self-Compassion:

Mindful Self-Compassion Practices:

Engaging in mindfulness exercises that specifically focus on self-compassion, such as loving-kindness meditation, allows individuals to cultivate a kind and accepting awareness of their thoughts and emotions.

Positive Affirmations:

Incorporating positive affirmations into daily life reinforces self-compassionate thinking. Affirmations that emphasize kindness, acceptance, and common humanity serve as powerful reminders of one's inherent worth.

Self-Reflective Journaling:

Journaling about personal experiences with a compassionate lens encourages self-reflection. Writing about challenges, acknowledging one's emotions, and exploring alternative, kinder perspectives contribute to self-compassion.

Self-Compassionate Language:

Paying attention to the language used towards oneself is crucial. Replacing self-critical thoughts with words of encouragement and understanding promotes a compassionate self-view.

Cultivating a Growth Mindset:

Embracing a growth mindset, which views challenges as opportunities for learning and growth, aligns with self-compassion. Individuals with a growth mindset see setbacks as part of the journey and approach them with a sense of kindness.

Seeking Professional Support:

Therapeutic interventions, such as cognitive-behavioral therapy (CBT) and mindfulness-based approaches, can provide tailored support in developing self-compassion. Mental health professionals offer guidance and tools for cultivating a compassionate self-view.

Challenges and Criticisms of Self-Compassion:

While the concept of self-compassion has gained widespread recognition, it is not without challenges and criticisms. Some individuals may find it difficult to adopt a self-compassionate mindset due to ingrained patterns of self-criticism or cultural influences that prioritize self-discipline over self-kindness. Additionally, critics argue that too much focus on self-compassion might lead to a lack of accountability or motivation. It is essential to acknowledge these perspectives while recognizing that a balanced approach to self-compassion can coexist with personal responsibility and growth.

Cultural and Societal Influences on Self-Compassion:

Cultural and societal factors play a significant role in shaping individuals' perceptions of self-compassion. In societies that prioritize individual achievement and self-reliance, the concept of self-compassion may face resistance. Cultural narratives that emphasize resilience, perseverance, and self-discipline may inadvertently discourage the practice of self-kindness. However, there is a growing recognition of the importance of integrating self-compassion into cultural discourse, as it aligns with a holistic understanding of well-being and mental health.

Embracing Gratitude for a Positive Perspective

Within the intricate web of human emotions, gratitude stands out as a potent element intertwining positivity, resilience, and a deep sense of well-being throughout the canvas of our existence. Embracing gratitude transcends a simple recognition of blessings; it entails fostering a mentality that actively seeks and values the positive facets of life. This thorough exploration delves into the diverse essence of gratitude, scrutinizing its psychological intricacies, practical implementations, and the profound influence it can wield on our outlook and overall satisfaction with life.

Understanding the Psychology of Gratitude:

Gratitude, from a psychological standpoint, is more than a polite thank you; it is a deep and genuine appreciation for the positive elements in our lives. Researchers such as Dr. Robert Emmons and Dr. Martin Seligman have explored the cognitive, emotional, and social dimensions of gratitude, identifying it as a key component of positive psychology. The core elements include:

Recognition of Blessings:

Gratitude involves recognizing and acknowledging the positive aspects of life, from small, everyday moments to significant milestones.

Appreciation for Others:

Expressing gratitude often involves recognizing the contributions and kindness of others, fostering a sense of connection and social bonds.

Enhanced Well-Being:

Numerous studies have linked gratitude to enhanced well-being, including improved mental health, increased life satisfaction, and a more optimistic outlook on the future.

Cultivation of Positive Emotions:

Gratitude is intertwined with positive emotions such as joy, contentment, and love. Actively practicing gratitude can contribute to a more positive emotional state.

Resilience in the Face of Challenges:

Individuals who embrace gratitude tend to exhibit greater resilience when faced with challenges. It acts as a buffer against stress and fosters adaptive coping mechanisms.

Practical Applications of Gratitude:

Gratitude Journaling:

Keeping a gratitude journal involves regularly writing down things for which one is thankful. This practice encourages reflection on positive experiences and cultivates a habit of focusing on the good in life.

Expressing Gratitude to Others:

Actively expressing gratitude to friends, family, colleagues, and even strangers can have a profound impact. Simple acts of thanking others contribute to positive social interactions and strengthen relationships.

Mindful Gratitude Practices:

Integrating gratitude into mindfulness practices enhances awareness of the present moment. Mindful gratitude involves savoring positive experiences and being fully present during moments of appreciation.

Gratitude Letters:

Writing letters expressing gratitude to individuals who have positively impacted one's life can be a transformative experience. Sharing these letters, if comfortable, strengthens social connections.

Gratitude in Adversity:

Embracing gratitude during challenging times involves reframing hardships and finding silver linings. It doesn't dismiss difficulties but encourages a perspective that acknowledges both struggles and the potential for growth.

Daily Gratitude Rituals:

Incorporating gratitude into daily routines, such as expressing thanks before meals or reflecting on positive moments before bedtime, establishes a consistent practice of acknowledging blessings.

Critiques and Considerations:

While the benefits of gratitude are well-documented, it is essential to acknowledge critiques and nuances surrounding its practice. Some individuals may find it challenging to embrace gratitude in the midst of adversity, as it may inadvertently invalidate genuine feelings of pain or sorrow. Additionally, a performative approach to gratitude, where individuals feel pressured to appear grateful, may undermine its authentic expression. Balancing the encouragement of gratitude with an understanding of its context and individual differences is crucial.

Cultural and Philosophical Perspectives on Gratitude:

Cultural and philosophical perspectives play a significant role in shaping attitudes towards gratitude. In cultures where communal values are emphasized, expressions of gratitude may be more communal and interconnected. Philosophical traditions, such as Stoicism and certain Eastern philosophies, incorporate gratitude as a fundamental aspect of virtue and contentment.

Embracing Gratitude for Positive Aging:

As individuals navigate the process of aging, embracing gratitude becomes particularly relevant. Gratitude can act as a guide for reframing perspectives on aging, focusing on the wisdom gained, meaningful connections, and the appreciation of life's journey.

Chapter 8: Empowering Your Mindset

Adopting a Growth Mindset

Within the realm of personal growth and accomplishment, embracing a growth mindset arises as a revolutionary philosophy with profound effects on learning, resilience, and overall success. Originating from the work of psychologist **Carol S. Dweck**, the notion of a growth mindset stands in opposition to a fixed mindset, asserting that capabilities and intelligence are malleable through commitment, persistence, and education. This in-depth investigation navigates the complexities of adopting a growth mindset, examining its psychological foundations, real-world implementations, and the crucial assessment of its influence on both individual and collective accomplishments.

Understanding the Fundamentals of a Growth Mindset:

At its core, a growth mindset hinges on the fundamental belief that one's abilities are not fixed traits but rather can be cultivated and enhanced over time. Individuals with a growth mindset perceive challenges as opportunities for growth, embrace effort as a path to mastery, and learn from criticism to improve. In contrast, a fixed mindset assumes that abilities are innate and unchangeable, leading to a desire to appear smart and a tendency to avoid challenges to maintain a sense of competence.

Psychological Underpinnings of a Growth Mindset:

Neuroplasticity and Learning:

Neuroscientific research supports the idea of neuroplasticity, indicating that the brain can adapt and rewire itself in response to learning and experiences. A growth mindset aligns with this concept, fostering a belief in the brain's malleability and its capacity for continuous development.

Motivation and Persistence:

Individuals with a growth mindset are more likely to approach tasks with enthusiasm and view setbacks as temporary obstacles. The belief that effort leads to improvement fuels motivation, encouraging perseverance in the face of challenges.

Embracing Challenges:

A growth mindset encourages the embrace of challenges as opportunities for learning and development. Instead of avoiding difficulties, individuals with a growth mindset see them as integral to the process of improvement.

Feedback as a Tool for Improvement:

Constructive feedback is welcomed in a growth mindset as it provides insights into areas that can be developed. Rather than taking feedback personally, individuals with a growth mindset see it as valuable information for refining their skills.

Practical Applications of a Growth Mindset:

Learning and Education:

In educational settings, fostering a growth mindset can have a profound impact on students' approach to learning. Teachers and parents can encourage the belief that intelligence is not fixed, promoting a love for learning and resilience in the face of academic challenges.

Professional Development:

In the workplace, a growth mindset is linked to increased adaptability, innovation, and a willingness to take on new responsibilities.

Organizations that cultivate a culture of continuous learning and improvement often see higher employee engagement and performance.

Relationships and Communication:

Adopting a growth mindset in interpersonal relationships involves seeing conflicts as opportunities for understanding and growth. It promotes effective communication by encouraging openness to different perspectives and a willingness to learn from others.

Leadership and Decision-Making:

Leaders with a growth mindset are more likely to foster a culture of innovation, resilience, and continuous improvement within their teams. The ability to see setbacks as learning experiences contributes to effective decision-making and problem-solving.

Critiques and Considerations:

While the benefits of a growth mindset are widely acknowledged, it is essential to consider potential critiques and nuances associated with its application. Critics argue that the emphasis on effort and growth may inadvertently downplay systemic barriers and inequalities. Additionally, a simplistic understanding of a growth mindset that ignores the role of external factors can lead to a reductionist view of achievement.

Cultural and Societal Perspectives:

Cultural and societal influences play a significant role in shaping attitudes towards a growth mindset. In cultures that value perseverance, learning, and improvement, the concept aligns seamlessly with existing values. However, in cultures that prioritize innate talent or fixed abilities, the adoption of a growth mindset may face resistance.

Overcoming Limiting Beliefs

On the path of personal growth, the powerful hurdles known as limiting beliefs pose a considerable threat to progress, acting as impediments that prevent individuals from unlocking their utmost potential. These beliefs, ingrained deeply in the subconscious, form self-imposed barriers that confine aspirations, limit actions, and cast shadows on overall life contentment. This in-depth exploration navigates the complexities of conquering limiting beliefs, meticulously examining their psychological origins, offering practical strategies, and critically assessing their profound influence on individual advancement and accomplishment.

Understanding Limiting Beliefs:

Limiting beliefs are deeply rooted convictions about oneself, others, or the world that impose restrictions on what is perceived as possible or achievable. These beliefs often stem from past experiences, societal influences, or repeated negative thoughts, shaping an individual's mindset and influencing decision-making.

Fixed Mindset vs. Growth Mindset:

One of the fundamental aspects of limiting beliefs is their alignment with a fixed mindset, as opposed to a growth mindset. A fixed mindset assumes that abilities and intelligence are static, leading to self-imposed limitations. Overcoming limiting beliefs often involves adopting a growth mindset, where individuals believe in their capacity for learning, improvement, and resilience.

Psychological Roots of Limiting Beliefs:

Early Childhood Experiences:

Limiting beliefs can originate from early childhood experiences, such as criticism, lack of encouragement, or perceived failures. These experiences create a foundation for negative self-perceptions that persist into adulthood.

Social Conditioning:

Societal norms, cultural expectations, and familial influences contribute to the formation of limiting beliefs. Messages received from external sources can shape an individual's worldview and beliefs about their capabilities.

Fear of Failure and Rejection:

The fear of failure or rejection can give rise to limiting beliefs about one's worthiness or ability to succeed. Individuals may avoid taking risks or pursuing opportunities due to the anticipation of negative outcomes.

Practical Strategies for Overcoming Limiting Beliefs:

Self-Awareness and Mindfulness:

The first step in overcoming limiting beliefs is cultivating self-awareness. Mindfulness practices, such as meditation and reflective journaling, provide individuals with the tools to observe their thoughts and identify patterns of limiting beliefs.

Cognitive Restructuring:

Cognitive restructuring involves challenging and reframing negative thoughts. By questioning the validity of limiting beliefs and replacing them with empowering and realistic alternatives, individuals can shift their perspective.

Affirmations and Positive Self-Talk:

Incorporating positive affirmations and engaging in constructive self-talk helps counteract limiting beliefs. By consistently reinforcing positive statements about oneself, individuals can reshape their self-image and build confidence.

Behavioral Exposure:

Gradual exposure to feared situations or challenges allows individuals to confront and overcome limiting beliefs through experience. This approach, often used in cognitive-behavioral therapy, encourages individuals to take small steps outside their comfort zones.

Seeking Support and Professional Help:

Sharing limiting beliefs with trusted friends, family, or a mental health professional provides external perspectives and support. Professional guidance can offer tailored strategies for challenging and overcoming deeply ingrained beliefs.

Increased Confidence and Self-Efficacy:

Overcoming limiting beliefs contributes to increased confidence and a sense of self-efficacy. As individuals challenge and conquer self-imposed limitations, they develop a greater belief in their ability to navigate challenges and achieve their goals.

Enhanced Resilience:

Resilience, the ability to bounce back from setbacks, is strengthened when limiting beliefs are addressed. Individuals become more adept at adapting to adversity and viewing failures as opportunities for growth rather than confirmation of limitations.

Improved Decision-Making:

Overcoming limiting beliefs allows for clearer thinking and more rational decision-making.

Individuals are better equipped to evaluate opportunities, take calculated risks, and pursue paths aligned with their values and aspirations.

Positive Impact on Mental Health:

The alleviation of limiting beliefs positively impacts mental health. Individuals may experience reduced stress, anxiety, and feelings of inadequacy as they break free from the constraints of self-limiting thoughts.

Critiques and Considerations:

While the importance of overcoming limiting beliefs is widely acknowledged, it is essential to recognize that the process is not always linear or without challenges. Some critics argue that an overly optimistic focus on positive thinking may oversimplify the complexities of addressing deeply rooted beliefs. Additionally, external factors such as systemic barriers and inequalities need to be acknowledged in discussions about overcoming limiting beliefs.

Balancing Work, Personal Life, and Self-Care

In the fast-paced and demanding landscape of modern life, achieving a harmonious balance between work responsibilities, personal life commitments, and self-care is a formidable challenge. The pursuit of equilibrium in these domains is a delicate art that requires thoughtful consideration, strategic planning, and a keen awareness of individual needs. This comprehensive analysis delves into the intricacies of balancing work, personal life, and self-care, critically examining the factors at play, proposing practical strategies, and evaluating the impact of this delicate equilibrium on overall well-being.

Understanding the Challenges:

Work-Driven Culture:

In a society often driven by career ambitions and productivity, individuals may find themselves immersed in a work culture that values constant output. The pressure to excel professionally can lead to neglect of personal and self-care aspects, creating an imbalance.

Technological Impact:

The advent of technology has blurred the boundaries between work and personal life. Constant connectivity through smartphones and emails can result in an inability to fully disengage from work, impacting personal time and self-care routines.

Individual Expectations:

Personal expectations and societal norms contribute to the challenges of balancing these aspects. Individuals may feel compelled to meet external standards, whether in their professional achievements or personal lives, often at the expense of self-care.

Critical Examination of Work-Life Integration:

Redefining Success:

A critical aspect of achieving balance involves redefining success. Rather than solely measuring success by professional achievements, individuals must include personal fulfillment and well-being as integral components of their definition of success.

Setting Boundaries:

Establishing clear boundaries between work and personal life is paramount. This includes delineating specific work hours, designating personal time, and learning to say no to excessive work demands.

Prioritizing Self-Care:

A critical component of balance is the prioritization of self-care. This involves recognizing the importance of physical and mental well-being, incorporating regular exercise, sufficient sleep, and activities that bring joy into daily routines.

Practical Strategies for Balance:

Time Management:

Effective time management is a cornerstone of achieving balance. Prioritizing tasks, setting realistic deadlines, and utilizing tools like calendars can help individuals allocate time efficiently across work, personal, and self-care domains.

Communication Skills:

Open and transparent communication is essential, both in the workplace and personal life. Clearly articulating boundaries, expectations, and needs fosters understanding and cooperation from colleagues, family, and friends.

Technology Detox:

Periodic breaks from technology, especially outside of work hours, can contribute to a healthier balance. Designating specific times for checking emails and disconnecting during personal or self-care moments helps establish boundaries.

Impact on Well-being:

Reduced Stress and Burnout:

Striking a balance between work, personal life, and self-care contributes to reduced stress and lowers the risk of burnout. It allows individuals to navigate challenges with resilience and maintain a sense of overall well-being.

Enhanced Productivity and Creativity:

A well-balanced life positively impacts professional performance. Adequate rest, recreation, and personal fulfillment enhance cognitive abilities, creativity, and productivity when engaged in work-related tasks.

Improved Relationships:

Balancing these aspects nurtures healthier relationships. Quality time spent with family and friends, as well as self-care practices, contribute to a more positive and fulfilling personal life, positively influencing interactions with others.

Considerations and Challenges:

Individual Variations:

Achieving balance is a highly individualized process. What works for one person may not be suitable for another. Understanding and respecting individual variations are crucial.

Flexibility and Adaptability:

The ability to adapt to changing circumstances and remain flexible in the approach to balance is vital. Life is dynamic, and strategies for balance may need adjustment over time.

Cultural and Organizational Influences:

Cultural norms and organizational cultures can significantly influence perceptions of balance. In some cultures or industries, long work hours may be the norm, impacting the perceived feasibility of achieving a balance.

Prioritizing Your Well-Being

Understanding Well-Being:

Well-being is a holistic concept that encompasses physical, mental, and emotional health, along with a sense of fulfillment and purpose in life. Prioritizing well-being involves recognizing its multifaceted nature and acknowledging its importance as a fundamental pillar of a fulfilling and meaningful existence.

Physical Well-Being:

This aspect encompasses aspects such as nutrition, exercise, and adequate sleep. Prioritizing physical well-being involves adopting habits that contribute to optimal bodily health, resilience, and vitality.

Mental and Emotional Well-Being:

Mental and emotional well-being involve cultivating a positive mindset, managing stress, and nurturing emotional resilience. Prioritizing this dimension is essential for maintaining psychological balance and coping effectively with life's challenges.

Social Well-Being:

Relationships and social connections are integral to well-being. Prioritizing social well-being involves fostering meaningful connections, maintaining healthy relationships, and engaging in supportive communities.

Factors Influencing Prioritization:

Cultural Influences:

Cultural norms and societal expectations can significantly impact how individuals prioritize well-being. In some cultures, there may be an emphasis on collective well-being, while in others, individual well-being may be emphasized.

Workplace Culture:

The culture within workplaces plays a pivotal role in influencing how individuals prioritize their well-being. Environments that promote a healthy work-life balance and prioritize employee well-being foster a conducive atmosphere for individuals to prioritize their own well-being.

Personal Values and Beliefs:

Individual values and belief systems shape the prioritization of well-being. Someone who values personal growth may prioritize activities that contribute to intellectual well-being, while someone valuing connection may prioritize social relationships.

The Intersection of Self-Care and Prioritizing Well-Being:

Self-Care Practices:

Self-care practices are integral to prioritizing well-being. These can include activities such as meditation, hobbies, or simply taking time for oneself. Understanding the importance of self-care is a foundational step in prioritizing overall well-being.

Setting Boundaries:

Prioritizing well-being often involves setting boundaries. This may include saying no to excessive commitments, establishing limits on work hours, and creating space for activities that contribute to one's well-being.

Mindful Decision-Making:

Being mindful of how decisions impact well-being is essential. Prioritizing well-being requires thoughtful decision-making that aligns with individual values and contributes positively to overall life satisfaction.

Practical Strategies for Prioritizing Well-Being:

Creating a Well-Being Plan:

Developing a well-being plan involves setting intentional goals and actionable steps to enhance various dimensions of well-being. This could include specific fitness routines, mindfulness practices, and strategies for maintaining healthy relationships.

Regular Self-Assessment:

Regular self-assessment involves reflective practices to evaluate one's well-being across different domains. This ongoing process allows individuals to identify areas that may need attention and make informed adjustments.

Seeking Professional Support:

Prioritizing well-being may involve seeking support from professionals, such as therapists, nutritionists, or fitness experts. These experts can provide tailored guidance to address specific well-being goals and challenges.

Impact of Prioritizing Well-Being:

Improved Physical Health:

Prioritizing well-being contributes to improved physical health. Healthy habits such as regular exercise, balanced nutrition, and sufficient sleep positively impact overall physical well-being.

Enhanced Mental Resilience:

Mental resilience is bolstered when individuals prioritize their well-being. Strategies such as stress management, mindfulness, and seeking support contribute to improved emotional and psychological well-being.

Increased Life Satisfaction:

Prioritizing well-being correlates with increased life satisfaction. When individuals intentionally invest in activities that bring joy, fulfillment, and a sense of purpose, overall life satisfaction is positively influenced.

Challenges and Considerations:

Balancing Priorities:

Balancing competing priorities can be challenging. Individuals may face dilemmas when trying to prioritize well-being alongside work, family, and other obligations. Finding a harmonious balance becomes crucial.

Cultural and Societal Pressures:

Cultural and societal pressures may discourage individuals from prioritizing their well-being. Overcoming external expectations and aligning actions with personal well-being goals may require intentional effort.

Consistency and Adaptability:

Prioritizing well-being is an ongoing journey that requires consistency and adaptability. Establishing sustainable habits and being open to adjusting practices as circumstances change are key considerations.

Conclusion: Your Personal Blueprint for Positivity

Reflecting on Your Journey

"Reflecting on Your Journey," individuals are encouraged to pause and introspect, extracting insights from the tapestry of their experiences. This act of self-reflection is a powerful compass, guiding through challenges, celebrating growth, and acknowledging resilience. Through retrospection, setbacks transform into stepping stones, offering profound lessons. Reflection isn't just a backward glance; it's a forward-thinking exercise, providing valuable insights for charting the course ahead. Cultivating gratitude and embracing the fluidity of growth, individuals navigate the cyclical nature of personal development. This chapter serves as a touchpoint in the perpetual journey of becoming, inviting intentional self-awareness and purposeful strides towards a future shaped by the wisdom gained through reflective exploration.

Sustaining Positive Change in the Long Run

It becomes evident that enduring transformation is not an isolated event but an ongoing, intentional journey. The essence lies in cultivating habits, fostering resilience, and embracing a mindset conducive to long-term well-being. Sustainable change involves embedding positive habits, creating a foundation for lasting transformation. Resilience emerges as the cornerstone, enabling individuals to navigate challenges with adaptability and fortitude. The mindset cultivated views change as a dynamic, lifelong process rather than a destination. Sustaining positive change is an ongoing commitment to self-discovery, continuous learning, and the unwavering belief that one can evolve positively over the course of a lifetime.